TULLAMORE

1 5 SEP 2023

WITHDRAWN

WHAT IF...

HUMANS WERE LIKE ANIMALS?

Concept and illustration by Paul Moran

Written by Lauren Taylor and Marianne Taylor
Edited by Lauren Taylor
Cover design by Angie Allison
Design by Barbara Ward

WHAT IF...
HUMANS WERE LIKE ANIMALS?

Buster Books

Leabharlann
Chontae Ulbh Fhaili

Class:
Acc.
Inv:

First published in Great Britain in 2013 by Buster Books,
an imprint of Michael O'Mara Books Limited,
9 Lion Yard, Tremadoc Road, London SW4 7NQ

www.busterbooks.co.uk

Text and illustrations copyright © Buster Books 2013

Additional illustration details from www.shutterstock.com

All rights reserved. No part of this publication may be reproduced, stored in
a retrieval system, or transmitted by any means, without the prior permission
in writing of the publisher, nor be otherwise circulated in any form of binding
or cover other than that in which it is published and without a similar condition
including this condition being imposed on the subsequent purchaser.

A CIP catalogue record for this book is available from the British Library.

ISBN: 978-1-78055-042-8 (in hardback format)
ISBN: 978-1-78055-117-3 (in ePub format)
ISBN: 978-1-78055-118-0 (in Mobipocket format)

2 4 6 8 10 9 7 5 3 1

Printed and bound in January 2013 by Clays Ltd,
St Ives plc, Popson Street, Bungay, Suffolk, NR35 1ED, UK

Papers used by Michael O'Mara Books are natural, recyclable products made
from wood grown in sustainable forests. The manufacturing processes conform to
the environmental regulations of the country of origin.

CONTENTS

What If ...

CONTENTS

... Humans Were Like Animals?

Do your parents ever complain that you're behaving like an animal? They usually mean that you are being untidy or eating with your mouth open, but what if humans really were like animals?

Did you know that voles eat their own young to make sure only the healthiest babies survive? If humans did this, you'd have to be really careful not to annoy your dad! But it's not all bad – there are plenty of amazing things you could do if you were like an animal. Turn the page to find out more, but before you do, check out the ratings below to tell the freaky from the fearsome and the useful from the yucky.

Beware a score of five – these creepy creatures are almost too scary to read about.

For the clever clogs of the animal world, a high score will leave you feeling dumbfounded.

A high score will make you wish for this fantastic animal feature, but a low score will have you thankful you're a human.

Encounter a score of five and you might have trouble keeping down your lunch.

... You Had Eyes On Your Hands?

If you are lucky, you have two eyes which your mum will probably tell you are beautiful. But what if you had eight eyes like a spider, or even a hundred like a scallop? Your mum would still love you, but other people might stare.

Handy Eyes

What if you had eyes on the ends of your arms like a starfish? Sure, it might be pretty gross to have eyeballs sticking out of the palms of your hands, but think how easily you could check around corners or read other people's magazines at the bus stop. You could even read two magazines at the same time if you felt like it.

HOW **4** HANDY

BUS STOP

One Hundred Peepers

Scallops are snail-like sea creatures. Some of them have a hundred eyes that they use to spot predators. If you had a hundred eyes you could watch TV, read this book, check your emails, stare out of the window and watch your own back, all at the same time.

A Real Eyeful

Here are some more eye-opening animal facts:

- An ostrich's eye weighs more than its brain.

- Some squid have eyes bigger than dinner plates.

- A fly has two eyes, but each contains thousands of lenses. That would look kind of creepy …

... Your Eyes Could Squirt Blood?

Could your eyes ever be gruesome enough to scare someone silly? It would be a cool trick if they were – though your victims might not agree. Here is an eye-popping animal trait you might find useful ...

Bursting Blood

A horned lizard can burst the blood vessels in its eyes, and shoot a stream of blood a distance of up to one and a half metres. Imagine trick-or-treating – you are dressed in your creepiest costume, your neighbour opens the door, you take aim and – BLAM – you squirt. Just make sure you get your hands on the sweets first, as people might not feel very generous when they're covered in blood.

... Your Eyes Were On One Side Of Your Head?

Eyes always come in very useful, no matter where they are on an animal's body. Your eyes are carefully positioned on your face so that you can see lots of things around you.

Eyes On The Side

Flatfish have both eyes on one side of their heads, so they can hide on the sea bed and still see. Great for a flatfish, but if you only had eyes on one side of your head, it would make it very easy for a thief to steal your wallet.

Fascinating, Freaky Fact

Hippos and crocodiles have eyes on top of their heads, so they can see above the water while hiding in it. Very useful for games of hide-and-seek.

... Your Ears Were Bigger Than Your Head?

Your ears aren't just for hearing, you probably think they are also useful for plugging in your headphones and holding up your sunglasses. But what if they had more interesting functions? Giant ears might look ridiculous, but they would keep you chilled in the heat of the sun.

Cooling Off

It can be scorching hot in Africa where some types of elephant live. One way elephants deal with the heat is flapping their large ears to keep cool. So forget an electric fan, just waggle your ears.

But what happens when your enormous ears get in the way? No problem ... just fold them up like the long-eared bat when you aren't using them.

Fascinating, Freaky Fact
Seals can close their ears to keep water out when they are swimming. So ditch your earplugs when diving for tasty fishy treats.

Did You Catch That?
Would you like to know when people are talking about you? All you'd need are ears twice as long as your head, like a jack rabbit's, and you would be able to hear every word. Huge ears might be a bit ear-ritating, but it's a small price to pay for supersonic hearing.

... Your Mouth Was On Your Stomach?

What if your mouth wasn't on your face? What if it was big enough to stuff in all your favourite foods at once?

A Feast Fit For A Starfish

If your mouth was where a starfish's mouth is, it'd be right in the middle of your body – on your stomach. You could munch away on a midnight feast while dozing off. Here's how:

1. Lean on a pile of pillows so you are sitting upright.

2. Make sure your stomach mouth has easy access to your favourite snacks, by laying them out nearby.

3. Now sleep tight and let your stomach bite. You might want to wear earplugs if the slurping noises get too loud.

ROTTEN
3
RATING

Open Wide

A basking shark has a gaping mouth big enough to fit two children inside. You might not fancy gobbling up two kids, but how about an entire birthday cake?

Just make sure you blow out the candles first ...

Forget The Bag

A pelican eel's mouth is more than three times wider than its body. If you had a mouth this big, you could carry around all your school stuff in there and not have to bother with a bag.

... You Never Had To Brush Your Teeth?

From never having to munch your meals again to never having to brush your teeth, seriously strange gnashers come in handy for all sorts of reasons.

Great Pearly Whites

Here are some excellent reasons to have teeth like a shark:

- If you lose any teeth, don't worry – they will be replaced by a brand new set! You could eat all the sweets and fizzy drinks you like and never have to brush your teeth.

- No dentist will want to come near you as your pearly whites would be super sharp.

- Whenever you want to frighten anyone, just give them your cheesiest toothy grin.

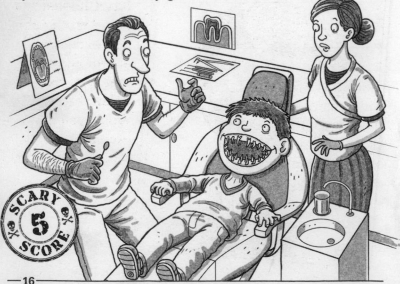

SCARY
5
SCORE

A Toothy Grin

A babirusa pig's upper teeth grow up instead of down, bursting right out of its face. If your teeth grew this way, you'd have a truly spectacular smile.

Say Cheese!

Sabre-tooth tigers, now extinct, had enormous fangs that grew well below their chins. Would you have liked these on school picture day?

... You Could Taste With Your Feet?

Do you love your food? If the answer is yes, think how cool it would be to taste or smell with other parts of your body – or even your whole body.

What A Feat!

What if you could taste with your feet like a butterfly? You could be chewing gum while tasting a cake recipe at the same time. The only problem is, would you really want to eat food that you'd trodden all over? If you serve the cake to your friends, just make sure you don't tell them that your stinky feet have been in it first.

ROTTEN
3
RATING

Tasty Bath

Catfish can smell and taste with their whole bodies. Just imagine, you could submerge yourself in a giant glass of cool lemonade on a hot day. Or if you're chocolate crazy, you could have your morning bath in warm chocolate sauce every day. Delicious!

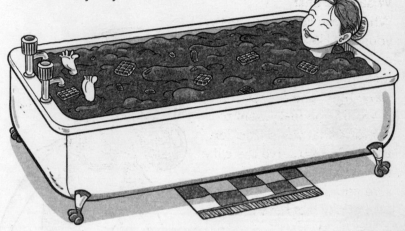

Smell It With Flowers

A snake smells the air with its tongue – the forked tip helps it work out where a smell is coming from. If this was the way your mum smelled, she'd wave her tongue around when you bought her flowers on Mother's Day.

... You Had Crazy Hair?

Most people have hair on their heads and some people have very long hair, but what if you were covered in long hair from top to toe?

Dreadful Locks

The Komodor is a dog breed that has floor-length dreadlocks all over its body. With hair like this, you definitely would be the coolest kid at the carnival.

Bottoms Up!

Hair is useful stuff – it can even keep you warm in cold weather, which would be great if you didn't wear clothes like an animal. Unfortunately, the mandrill is out of luck. This is a type of large, hairy monkey with a colourful, but very bare, bottom. Being covered in hair might be toasty warm, but you'd have a very chilly bum.

Heaps Of Hair

If you're lucky, you might wake up one day with hair like a musk ox, the hairiest of any animal. With 60-centimetre-long hair all over your body, you could rock several amazing hairstyles all at once – pigtails, plaits, kiss-curls and a spiky mohawk. The downside is that your hair would be really annoying to wash and brush every day, and imagine how blocked the plughole in your bath would get from all that hair. Gross!

Fascinating Furry Facts

Take a look at these hair-raising facts:

- There is a breed of dog called an American hairless terrier and a breed of cat called a Sphynx that have no fur at all.

- Sea otters have an amazing 100,000 hairs per square centimetres of skin.

- Polar bears actually have colourless fur, but it reflects the light to make it appear white.

... Your Skin Could Change Colour?

Some people change the colour of their hair to all kinds of wacky, bright shades, but you're pretty much stuck with the colour of your skin. What if you weren't?

Hide-And-Seek

Some octopuses can change the colour and pattern on their skin to match whatever's around them. If you had the power to change your skin, you could hide against brick walls or bookshelves and become a very successful top-secret spy. Why stop there? You could sneak into the cinema for free by hiding in front of movie posters.

ROTTEN 2 RATING

Sharp As A Shark

A shark's skin is covered with 'dermal denticles'. These are hard spikes that are made of the same stuff as teeth. If you had teeth all over your skin, you might shave all the hair off your dog by just brushing past him.

Skin For Rainy Days

Lizards called frilled dragons each have a huge crest of colourful skin around their necks, five times wider than their faces. The crests look rather like upturned umbrellas, which wouldn't be very useful on a rainy day.

... You Had Two Heads?

You know what they say – two heads are better than one.
This isn't just a clever saying, it's almost true for some
amazing animals.

Sleepy Head

A yellow-lipped sea krait
snake has a tail that looks
exactly like its head to fool
predators. If you had a trick
head, you could take a
snooze with your real head
and keep the other looking
bright and alert in class
– no one would ever know
the difference.

One Step Ahead

What if your parents appeared to have two pairs of eyes?
Some birds have eye-like patterns on the backs of their
heads, so it seems like they're watching you when they're
not. Your devious deeds might come to an end if you
could never be sure if you were being watched or not.

Tusk Tricks

Would you like a long tusk on your face like a male narwhal (a kind of whale)? You could pop marshmallows on the end to roast over the campfire. Toasty!

Head Check

Check out your head in the mirror, and see how many of these fantastic features you have. If you can't check off any, chances are you're just a human.

☐ A stalk with a dangling light on the end to attract prey, like the anglerfish.

☐ Magnetic particles in your head to help you navigate, like a pigeon.

☐ No head at all! A chicken called Mike from Colorado, US, lived without a head for 18 months.

☐ A bulgy forehead like a dolphin to conduct sound waves, allowing you to hear underwater.

... You Could Crush Ribs With A Hug?

Arms are useful things – you can reach for a snack or hug your little brother (when you feel like it), but what if your arms had super strength or you had more than two of them?

Crushing Cuddles

The arms of a male chimpanzee are an amazing five times stronger than those of a man, and a big male mountain gorilla has a whopping two-and-a-half-metre arm span. If your mum had the arm strength of a chimp and the mega arm span of a gorilla, not only could she sweep you and all your brothers and sisters up in one big hug, she would probably give you all a good crushing if she was too enthusiastic.

HOW
1
HANDY

Flying Underwater

Swimming can be tough work. If you had flippers like a penguin, you would glide through the water like a bird flying through the air. Catching a tasty fish for your supper would be a breeze.

Barmy Army

If two arms aren't enough to do all the things you'd like to be able to do, how would you like eight arms like an octopus? Better still, your arms would be covered in grippy suckers to cling on to things. You could play a computer game, comb your hair, lift weights and brush your teeth all at the same time.

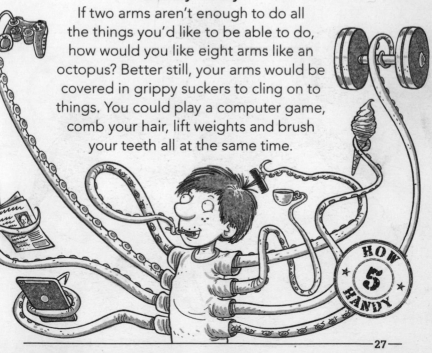

HOW
5
HANDY

... You Grew More Legs As You Got Older?

You might think you get through life fine with only two legs, but what if you had four, or six, or even hundreds? Or what if you had legs longer than anyone else you knew?

Loads Of Legs

Millipedes and centipedes are well known for having many legs. But did you know they grow more legs the older they get? If you sprouted a new pair of legs for every birthday you'd get a great deal of shoes for presents. And you'd really need them – especially if you were a rare type of Californian millipede that has a whopping 750 legs.

HOW 4 HANDY

Lengthy Legs

Black-winged stilts are birds with legs one and a half times longer than the rest of their bodies. If you had such fantastically long legs, you'd be first pick for the basketball team – the only player who could make a slam dunk without jumping. Unfortunately, off the basketball court, you'd spend a great deal of time talking to the tops of people's heads.

... You Could Hang From The Ceiling?

Many people think human feet are stinky and gross, but if human feet had some of these useful features, people might learn to love them.

Let's Hang Out

If you had feet like a sucker-footed bat you could hang upside-down from the ceiling without falling, thanks to suction pads on your feet. You could be generous and offer to help your dad paint the ceiling, or if you were feeling particularly mischievous you could simply drop water balloons on your unsuspecting family.

A Pongy Pair

When dogs sweat nearly all of it comes out of their feet. Feet are pretty pongy to begin with – how would you keep the stink at bay if you sweated in the same way?

ROTTEN
4
RATING

Famished Feet

Some feet aren't just used to walk on. Horseshoe crabs use their spiny feet as teeth, to 'chew' their food. Imagine having to chew everything with your feet before putting it in your mouth. Your parents wouldn't be too happy if you had to get your feet out at the dinner table. They might also make you floss between your toes. Yuck!

... You Had A Fly-Swatting Tail?

Many animals have tails. It's a little unfair that we humans don't, as they would come in useful when you want to do something that arms and legs just can't handle.

Why Would You Want A Tail?

From swinging in the trees to swatting flies, there are a lot of reasons why a tail would come in handy.

- If you were a lizard, your tail would break off if a predator grabbed it, leaving you free to escape.

- Summertime picnics can be surrounded by buzzing flies. If you had a fly-swatting tail like a cow, one swift whip would show them who's boss.

HOW 4 HANDY

- If you had a tail like most monkeys, you'd feel at home swinging care-free in the tree tops. You'd also have somewhere to hide when your mum started bugging you to do your homework.

- If you were a squirrel, you wouldn't need a blanket to keep you warm while you slept – just wrap yourself in your cosy, bushy tail.

- Komodo dragons knock their prey down with their powerful tails. You might not have to catch your own food, but you could use a tail like this to take a swipe at someone helping themselves to a tasty treat you had your eye on.

... You Were Leafy Like A Tree?

Have you ever wished you had a crazy body part to stand out from the crowd? Would having a see-through head make you the envy of all your friends or would they just call you an airhead?

Make Like A Tree And Leave

A leafy sea dragon is a weird fish with what looks like leaves growing out of its body. When it's floating around in the ocean, it looks just like a piece of seaweed. This look could work perfectly well for you, too. If you had these useful leafy adornments, you could hang out in the park all day. No one would suspect that that odd-looking tree was bunking off school.

What An Airhead!

There is a deep-sea fish, called *Macropinna microstoma*, which has a see-through head. Pretty cool, wouldn't you say? Unless your friends started to have a conversation while looking right through you – very rude!

ROTTEN
4
RATING

Tentacle-Tastic

If you had the tickly 35-metre-long sticky tentacles of a lion's mane jellyfish, you could:

- Torture your sister by tickling her like crazy.

- Become the world's speediest hairdresser.

- Tie both your shoelaces at the same time.

- Dip your sticky tentacles in a jar of sweets and lick them off – yum!

... You Had Pop-Up Claws?

Do you ever wish you had a built-in weapon with which to freak out your parents? What if you had claws on your hands or a saw for a nose? Getting out of housework would be a breeze.

A Wicked Weapon

Not only is a hairy frog quite hairy, which is odd enough for a frog, it also has sharp claws under its skin that pop out of its 'fingertips' when it's feeling particularly moody. With an instant weapon like this, you would be well on your way to becoming a superhero and your mum would never make you tidy your room again.

On Guard!

A male Hercules beetle has a big, pointy horn that he uses to fight other Hercules beetles. Arguments about who gets to use the bathroom first could get nasty.

Slice And Dice

Sawfish get their name because they have long, flat noses with little spikes along the edges. If you had this handy tool attached to your face, you wouldn't necessarily have to use it for fighting. You could be a great help to your parents, slicing and dicing the vegetables for dinnertime. Just watch out where you're pointing that thing ...

HOW HANDY 3

... You Had A Killer Kick?

It would be nifty to have a superhero's skills to fight crime and beat the baddies. Which of these animal powers would you like to have?

The Killer Kicker

If you could kick like a horse, you could strike an attacker with the force of a bowling ball travelling at 130 kilometres an hour. One blow would send the thug flying so far he'd never bother you again.

The Beaked Beater

If you had the dagger-like beak of a heron, you could spear bag-snatchers in one swift swoop.

SCARY
4
SCORE

Python Man

A large python can disable its prey by squashing them in its coils. If you had this squeezing strength, you could tie up villains in your coils.

More Marvellous Superpowers

The fun doesn't stop there. Check out some of these scary talents.

- **The Spurred Avenger**
  Male platypuses have venom-filled spurs (sharp, horny growths) on their back legs.

- **The Spiked Assassin**
  Porcupines can run backwards to skewer predators on their 35-centimetre quills.

- **Captain Venom**
  One bite from an inland taipan snake contains enough venom to kill more than 100 people.

- **Bullet Boy**
  Being stung by a bullet ant is as painful as being shot with a real bullet.

... You Had Super-Smelly Self-Defence Skills?

Survival skills can be violent, clever, quick ... or smelly. But no matter how repulsive they are, if your defence skills are successful, no attacker will want to come near you again.

Skunk Attack

Skunks scare off predators by squirting them with a horrible-smelling liquid from a gland on their bottoms – disgusting but completely effective.

If you ever had to use this gross tactic, you could run away, safe in the knowledge your attacker would smell disgusting for days to come.

Puke Patrol

If predators come too close to the nest of a type of seabird, called a fulmar, it vomits fishy gunk over them. This would make a great neighbourhood-watch tactic for humans. You could simply hide in a tree and vomit on thieves below to deter them.

ROTTEN **4** RATING

Ka-Boom!

Asian termites stop predatory insects entering their tunnels by blowing themselves up and blocking the way with their gooey insides. This is not recommended for humans – you might save your house, but you'd be a bit dead.

... You Looked Like A Pine Cone?

Some animals have terrific hiding skills to protect them from predators. What if you could disguise yourself from being seen?

Camouflage Charge

Pangolins are African anteaters that are covered in large scales that make them look like pine cones. You might not like the idea of having rough, scaly skin, but you could happily hide nestled in a leafy forest. You'd also have wicked armour should you ever need to leap out on your enemy and take them by surprise. What's more, pangolins can also emit a foul smelling acid from their bottoms. Bonus!

Disgusting Disguise

If you're really desperate for a disguise, do as the larva (worm-like baby insects) of the lily beetle does, and give yourself a generous coating of your own poo. This would be very useful when hiding in muddy forests, although a bit smelly.

What A Fluke!

The idea of camouflage is, of course, that you can hide from things you don't want to find you. Strangely, fish that are infected with flukes (a type of parasite) sometimes go a bit bonkers and start showing off in front of a predator rather than hiding from it. If you had a nasty case of flukes you might suddenly decide that doing cartwheels in front of a lion is an excellent idea.

... You Lived In A Mound Of Poo?

Luckily, you have warm clothes and a roof over your head – usually provided by your parents. But out in the wild, animals have to make their own living arrangements.

Do-It-Yourself

If you were a termite, it would be easy to build your own house. All you would need is some chewed-up wood, a little mud and a generous helping of poo. This is how termites build their mounds, which can be a whopping nine metres high. This is the equivalent of building a house over 3,000 metres high for a human. That's about as high as a mountain.

ROTTEN **5** RATING

Home Sweet Home

Tree houses can be fun to play around in, but would you fancy living in a tree full time? Sociable weavers (sparrow-like birds) make huge communal nests that look like haystacks and take up entire trees. Tree-top living might sound ideal, but you're likely to get quite soggy when it rains.

SMART 5 POINTS

Forest Fashions

Tailorbirds build their nests by sewing two leaves together, using plant fibres as threads and their beaks as needles. If you had these sewing skills, you could make all your own clothes.

... You Made Sticky Slime?

Some animals have the ability to make amazing things. Of course, these skills are very useful to the animals, but for humans, how handy would it be?

Stuck Like Glue

Mussels make a glue-like substance to help them cling on to things, such as the bottoms of ships and rocks. Just one smear of this super-sticky stuff is enough to keep them stuck for over 50 years. Just imagine, if a person could produce this gluey stuff and accidentally stuck themselves to the ceiling, they might well be stuck there until they were old and wrinkly.

Caterpillar Costumes

Many people consider silk to be a very elegant fabric, but did you know it comes from glands inside a caterpillar's mouth? It could be a little embarrassing if you suddenly started spewing out strands of silk from your mouth, but just consider other possibilities. You could ...

- offer your services to a dressmaker – you might even get some fashionable freebies

- spin webs like a spider to catch any pesky flies in your house

- swing from the rooftops like a superhero, using home-made ropes of silk.

HOW
3
HANDY

... You Could Lift A Truck?

There are lots of animals that can lift far more than their own body weight. The Hercules beetle, for example, can lift an amazing 850 times its own weight.

Heavyweights

If you could lift as much as the Hercules beetle relative to your body weight, it would be like lifting 65,000 kilograms – that's not just one truck, but several. The most a man has ever lifted is a measly 263 kilograms. Here are some other amazingly heavy things you could lift:

- a baby blue whale
- 30,000 bricks
- 10 Tyrannosaurus rex
- over 200,000 toilet rolls
- a fighter jet
- a double decker bus
- a million chocolate bars
- 2,500 poodles.

Flying Fit

Do you have a lot of heavy books to carry to school? This would be no problem if you were an eagle. You could just fly, skipping the traffic jams and you'd also have the strength to carry a bag that weighs half your own weight with your feet.

Champion Chewers

A spotted hyena's jaws are strong enough to chew up a saucepan. If you had these mega-strength jaws and were still peckish after your dinner, you could just munch on the saucepan it was cooked in – one less thing to wash up. Hyenas don't eat saucepans, of course. Instead they use their jaws to crush animal bones.

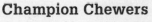

WHAT IF ...

... You Were As Fast As A Cheetah?

How would you like to run across a country in a couple of days or out swim a motor boat? The super speed of some animals is enough to leave you breathless.

Rapid Runners

A cheetah can dash at a spectacular 100 kilometres an hour. If you could maintain such an awesome speed, you could run across the United States of America in under two days. You couldn't slow down or take a break, of course, so you'd need to take a whole lot of water with you.

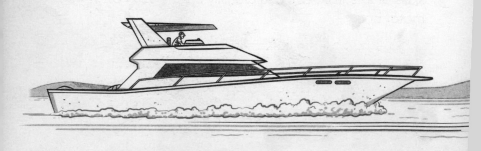

Perfect Pecker

Woodpeckers can strike a tree at a rate of 22 pecks a second. If you were lucky enough to have a beak and be such a nifty pecker, your skills would make you the envy of everyone in wood-working class.

Swift Swimmers

The fastest fish around is a sailfish, which can zoom through the water at a speedy 110 kilometres an hour. As its name suggests, this super-quick fish has a large fin on its back that sticks up like a sail. If you had the swimming skills of a sailfish, you could easily out swim an average motor boat.

... You Could Jump Over A Skyscraper?

You may have tried your hand at high jump at school, or maybe even seen Olympic athletes do it, but that is nothing compared to the heights that some animals can reach.

Jumping Journeys

There is a small insect called a froghopper that can jump 70 centimetres straight up in the air. That might not sound terribly high, but the equivalent for a person would mean leaping over a skyscraper. Getting to work every morning would be easy – and a lot more fun than driving a car.

HOW **4** HANDY

Aim High

Serval cats can jump three metres in the air to grab passing birds. This is the equivalent of a human jumping almost five metres. If you had the super-jumping skills of a serval, you'd be sure to win a gold medal. You wouldn't have to grab a bird on your way up – unless you really wanted to.

Leap Of Faith

The day after baby wood ducks hatch, they have to jump out of the tree where their nest is before they can fly. If they are lucky, they get a soft landing and don't hurt themselves.

... You Could Climb Up Windows?

Unless you're a daredevil rock climber, you probably spend most of your time walking around on the ground. However, for some climbing critters, the ground is old news.

Fly Feet

Flies have tiny hairs on their feet which make them ultra grippy. They can even walk on windows by gripping on to the glass. In case you ever find yourself with such a super ability, here some dos and don'ts:

DO

- Make sure your neighbours are out before you climb up their windows.

- Wear a helmet if you plan to climb very high.

- Be wary of low-flying planes.

DON'T

- Wear shoes, or the hairs on your feet won't work.

- Jump! Gravity doesn't work that way – you'll only go down.

- Be surprised if your parents ground you – literally!

Great Geckos

If you could walk up and down walls like a gecko (a type of small lizard), the need for ladders would be a thing of the past. You could make a lot of money with your own painting and decorating company, as wallpapering a room would be a breeze.

HOW
4
HANDY

Scale With Scales

Many snakes are skilled climbers, gripping surfaces with the raised scales on their bellies. If you had these climbing scales, you could go rock climbing without the safety ropes – what a daredevil!

... You Could Survive Sub-Zero Temperatures?

When it's cold outside, you probably have to bundle up to keep warm. But what if you could survive whatever the weather?

Frozen Solid
Woolly bear caterpillars in the Arctic spend ten months of the year frozen solid. If you did this, you'd only have two months in a year to do all your school work!

Out Of This World
Tardigrades are microscopic creatures that can cope with temperatures from as low as −273°C and as high as 151°C. They can even survive in outer space. If you were this robust, you could take a holiday that would be literally out of this world. All you'd need to do is hitch a ride on a rocket ship.

Thanks, Dad!

How would you feel about standing outside in −40°C for 64 days? You probably wouldn't jump at the chance, but male emperor penguins do this every year while looking after an egg between their legs while their mates go in search of food. Would you fancy being crammed between your dad's knees for over two months in the freezing cold?

So, You Want To Live Like A Penguin?

Here are some of the other crazy things you'd have to do if you lived like a penguin in freezing Antarctica.

- Huddle together for warmth with your massive group of penguin friends — up to several hundred.

- Be careful not to fall out of your dad's brood patch — a featherless patch of warm skin — you'd freeze to death in a matter of minutes.

- Dive for food to depths of over 550 metres in the freezing Antarctic waters.

- Eat food regurgitated, or puked up, by your mum and dad. Yum!

... You Could Fly As High As A Plane?

If beating a world record is on the top of your to-do list, take a look at some of these strange animal records. They might just give you some inspiration.

Highest Flier
The ability to fly is probably at the top of a lot of people's wish lists, but it doesn't come without its perils. The highest-flying bird on record is a vulture. It hit a plane that was flying at 11,277 metres high. Ouch!

Longest-Lived

It's possible that bowhead whales can live for over 200 years, making them the longest-lived mammals on the planet. If you could reach this age, your birthday cake would have to be massive to hold all the candles. Would you have enough puff left to blow them all out?

Longest Tongue

A chameleon's tongue can be up to twice the length of its body. It can whip out of its mouth in a speedy 0.7 seconds to snatch up prey. You could easily snap up that last slice of cake without anyone noticing.

HOW **3** HANDY

... You Couldn't Speak?

If you didn't communicate by talking, you might wonder how on earth you'd get your point across. It turns out that animals have some of the strangest ways of 'speaking' that you can imagine.

Could You Repeat That?

If you didn't have a voice, you might like to try communicating like a grasshopper. Grasshoppers rub their legs against their abdomens to make the chirps they use to 'speak' to each other. The only problem is, no one would understand what you were saying – apart from grasshoppers, that is!

HOW **1** HANDY

Take A Bow

What if you saw little kids politely bowing to each other in the playground? This is what dogs do when they want to play – they bow deeply to each other. How polite!

On The Trail

Termites leave a scent trail to tell each other where to find food. If you could do this, you'd certainly be very popular with all your friends, but you'd have to make sure you got to the food first before the others ate all the best bits.

... Life Was A Musical?

If humans communicated like animals, everyday life would become very exciting and strange. You'd certainly never be bored.

A Whale Of A Time

Whales communicate with song, even though their clicks, squeals and long, drawn-out groans may not sound very musical to us. If all your teachers taught their lessons in song, school would be a lot more lively, don't you think? And by whale-singing standards, it wouldn't even matter if they couldn't sing very well.

Light Entertainment

A firefly squid can light up parts of its body to impress other firefly squids. If you and your friends could do this, you could communicate secretly in the dark with Morse code.

HOW HANDY 3

Say What?

Animals communicate in so many different ways. There are probably just as many different types of 'talking' as there are animals on the planet.

- Nightjars are birds that fly at night. They signal in the dark by flashing their white wing feathers at each other. You can confuse a nightjar by waving a white hankie in the air.

- Birds migrating at night twitter constantly, so no one gets separated from the group.

- Howler monkeys communicate with blood-curdling screeches. I bet your teachers are very glad this isn't the way you and your friends chat to each other.

- Prairie dogs (a type of rodent) squeak to warn each other of danger. The pitches of the squeaks let others know exactly how scary the situation is.

... You Fell In Love With Farts?

Most people consider farting rude, smelly and something that should be avoided in public at all costs, but some animals are unashamed of their tremendous gases.

Fabulous Farts

Farts – they are wonderful things if you're a southern pine beetle. The smell of the female beetle's farts is highly attractive to a male. So, ladies, forget this season's perfume or that expensive bubble bath, all you need is what nature gave you – a healthy dose of digestive gas.

ROTTEN
3
RATING

Speak Fart

Some fish may use farts to communicate with each other. Would you swap learning French or Spanish for a lesson in the fine art of farting if humans did the same thing?

SMART 3 POINTS

Wipe Out

Dogs' digestive systems can't digest fart-tastic beans very well. If you had the gut of a dog and ate a plate of beans, you would fart huge volumes of gas – maybe enough to wipe out a lift full of people in one go.

... You Walked Upside Down?

It's no fun being ill, but there are some ghastly diseases that affect animals in strange and intriguing ways.

Handy Standing

A swim bladder is an organ in a fish that helps it to stay afloat in water. A fish with a diseased swim bladder will often swim upside-down. If a person could catch this condition, they might walk upside-down, on their hands. On the bright side, if you ever feel like joining the circus, you'd have no problem finding a job.

Hold Still ...

Some animal diseases might sound cool and fairly harmless, but there are others you'll want to avoid like the plague. Sadly, when bee larvae pick up a fungal disease called stonebrood, it causes the soft and squishy larvae to turn hard like stones, almost like they've been mummified. If you were in danger of turning to stone, not only would it be terrifying, it could also be really embarrassing. What if you were stuck while picking your nose, sniffing your armpits or something equally cringe-worthy?

... You Had A Parasite For A Tongue?

When you're being annoying, your big brother or sister might call you a 'parasite', which is a creature that will use another living thing for food and protection all its life.

Lick With A Woodlouse

The spotted rose snapper fish can suffer from a woodlouse-like parasite that destroys its tongue. Eventually the fish uses the parasite as a replacement tongue. If this happened to you it would be pretty disgusting, plus you wouldn't even be able to taste your food.

Tropical Vampires

Mockingbirds in the Galápagos islands peck holes in the skin of sea lions to drink their blood. Forget about going to the beach to have a relaxing sunbathe!

Nutrients Nabbers

Believe it or not, some pesky parasites steal the nutrients animals get from their food. Male angler fish attach themselves to the much larger female angler fish and absorb nutrients from them. If human males were parasites like this, imagine how annoying it would be if you were just popping out to the shops and were bombarded by a horde of tiny men, trying to nab your nutrients.

ROTTEN 4 RATING

... You Could Eat Rocks For Breakfast?

Do you think you have a strong stomach? Maybe you can gobble down a fiery hot curry without breaking a sweat, but are your guts tough enough to handle a diet of rocks?

Rock 'n' Rolls

Ostriches have the perfect solution for a spot of indigestion. They simply swallow a bunch of grit and rocks, that sit in their stomach and help grind up the tough plants they eat. This might come in handy when you want to scoff yourself silly at a barbecue, but you'd probably break a few of your teeth trying to munch on rocks afterwards.

... Your Guts Were On Show?

Usually, guts are neatly tucked away inside the human body, but what if they were on show for the world to see? Yuck!

Weird Windpipes

Ever bitten off more than you can chew – literally? If you were like some snakes, you'd be able to pop your windpipe out of your mouth, to make room to swallow massive things. Some snakes like to swallow whole deer, but maybe you'd prefer to stick with a tasty burger.

X-tra Special

The X-ray tetra fish has a see-through body, so you can see all of its inner workings. If you were transparent, everyone would be able to see what you'd just eaten for lunch.

ROTTEN 4 RATING

... You Ate 850 Sausages In One Go?

If you love stuffing yourself silly, you might like to have a huge stomach like a blue whale. You'd never feel full.

Meaty Menu

A lion can scoff 34 kilograms of meat in one go. Here's what might be on the menu if you could undertake such a meaty meal:

- 850 sausages or barbecue ribs
- 220 steaks or pork chops
- 24 roast chickens
- 1,500 meatballs.

Aren't You Full Yet?

Do your parents ever tell you off for bolting down your food? They should be pleased they don't have a giant panda for a child who does the opposite. A giant panda will spend 15 hours a day just munching bamboo.

Get Your Fill Of Krill

Blue whales feed almost entirely on tiny shrimp-like sea animals called krill, and can get through 40 million of them every day. If you had to eat only one thing – and this much of it – the very idea of eating might bore your brains out.

ROTTEN 2 RATING

... You Could Tackle A Lioness?

Hopefully you've never eaten anything bigger than can fit on a dinner plate. But what if you could devour something twice your size and still feel hungry the next day?

A Lion For Lunch

Stoats regularly catch and eat rabbits more than twice as big as them. Rabbits may not be particularly ferocious, but size-wise this is about the same as a fully grown man munching on a lioness. Would you be brave enough to give it a go, or would you rather leave it to your dad?

SCARY 5 SCORE

Super Swallower

If you were a black swallower fish you could swallow something up to ten times your weight – whole! Your stomach would be able to expand to fit it in, but you might not be able to fit into your trousers.

Outside In

A hagfish chews its way into larger fish, then eats them from the inside. If you were a hagfish, instead of getting a tasty steak on your plate, you'd have to eat your way into a cow to get it.

… You Ate A Plate Of Jellyfish?

From poisonous jellyfish to steering wheels, animals have been known to munch on mysterious things. Would you have the appetite for any of these snacks?

Jelly Belly

Sea turtles happily eat jellyfish, stinging tentacles and all. Usually this sort of crazy behaviour would be deadly for a human, but if you had a sea turtle's strong stomach, you could add a dash of sauce and a generous helping of meatballs to your jellyfish dish. It might look no different to a big plate of spaghetti.

ROTTEN
4
RATING

Tasty Trees

Elephants eat the wood and bark of trees as well as the leaves. If such a treat tickled your fancy, and your stomach could digest it, you could forget taking a picnic to the park and just munch on the nearby trees!

Bins With Fins

Tiger sharks are known as 'bins with fins' because they will eat everything and anything they encounter, even swallowing inedible objects. Fancy chowing down on a steering wheel, anyone?

... Your Mum Puked In Your Mouth?

Animals can do some pretty disgusting things, but *eating* gross things might be one step too far. You'd have to be starving to indulge in some of these sickening snacks.

Vile Vomit

Some mother birds feed their babies by eating the food first then vomiting it back up into their little one's mouth. It's called regurgitation. Human babies need feeding more frequently than adults, so if your mum fed you like this that would be a whole lot of puking. If she fed you what birds eat, here are some of the things you might have to force down:

- seeds and berries
- raw fish
- a ball of insects, called a bolus
- worms.

ROTTEN **5** RATING

Fine Dining ...
Down The Toilet

Magpie birds regularly pick through piles of animal poo, looking for undigested food. If you did the same, you'd have to eat all your meals in the toilet and would probably become seriously ill from all the nasty bacteria.

Brains, Anyone?

In a remote cave in Hungary, scientists discovered that a group of small birds called great tits got so hungry they visited a bat roost and pecked the sleeping bats' brains out. What if, feeling like a midnight snack, you popped over to your friend's house to tuck into their brain? You probably wouldn't be invited round again.

... Someone Drank Your Sweat?

There's nothing better than a cool drink on a hot day, unless of course that drink happens to be human sweat ...

Stinking Drinking

Sweat bees live in hot countries and land on people's face to drink their sweat. What if every time you got a bit hot and sweaty, you had to fend off other people swooping in for a tasty lick? Sports day at school would be a nightmare.

ROTTEN
5
RATING

... Someone Ate Your Skin?

Most humans don't think twice about eating animals. Many animals, such as mosquitos, feel exactly the same about nibbling unsuspecting humans.

A Flaky Feast

Imagine snuggling into bed one night and suddenly discovering your little brother beneath your covers, nibbling on your dead flakes of skin. This is what dust mites do. It would be hard to sleep after this disgusting discovery.

Goochy Goochy – Ouch!

Imagine if human babies had the bone-crushing bite of a snapping turtle. These creatures have very strong jaws and wouldn't think twice about snipping your finger clean off.

... You Drank Over A Hundred Litres Of Water?

You might not think there's much to drinking other than gulping down a glass of your favourite juice or fizzy drink. However, for animals, the art of drinking can be much more creative than that.

Thirsty Work

Drinking is thirsty work, especially if you're a camel that can gulp down over 100 litres of water in one go and then not have to drink again for over a week. If you had this ability, you would make a great desert-rescue hero for stranded travellers.

Make A Splash

Drinking like an elephant would be great fun. They suck water into their trunks, then squirt it into their mouths. Water fight!

Fantastic Drinking Facts

Do you think all animals drink plain water?
Think again …

- Seabirds drink sea water, but get rid of the excess salt through their nostrils.

- Some butterflies drink juices from animal droppings.

- When there's nothing to drink, some lizards re-absorb water from the urine in their bladders.

- Malaysian tree shrews drink alcoholic nectar – the equivalent of nine glasses of strong beer a day.

... You Wrestled With Your Food?

Some people like to eat meat that is nearly raw. But how about so raw it can still moo? If people ate their food while it was still alive like some animals do, the world would be a wilder place.

Rip 'n' Roll

Crocodiles rip bits off creatures while they're still alive by violently shaking and rolling about. This is called a death roll. It's rather like wrestling – with a violent twist. If you had to go through this ordeal with a cow every time you wanted a beef burger, you might very well become a vegetarian.

HOW
1
HANDY

Talking Food

Grass snakes swallow frogs whole, and these frogs can sometimes be heard squealing for several minutes after they've been eaten. If this happened to you, it would be far more embarrassing than your stomach grumbling loudly.

IT'S DARK IN HERE!

Chase Down Your Chow

Orcas (also known as killer whales) take bites out of their prey while chasing it. If you really feel you must chase down your dinner in this way, remember to take these essentials along with you:

- When chasing sheep, take dental floss to remove the wool from your teeth.

- If you're going pig chasing, wear wellies – you're likely to be trawling through some muddy areas.

- If you're chasing birds, good luck, unless you have wings!

... You Had To Dance For Your Dinner?

If you had to catch your own food, you might have to do any number of crazy things to lure it to you – some more strange than others ...

Shall We Dance?

What if dancing wasn't just a fun thing to do, but essential for your survival? Weasels are said to perform a hypnotising 'dance' to confuse their prey before they pounce. Imagine if your parents made you dance for your dinner every day? Cringe!

The Webbed Assassin

One kind of assassin bug will ping the webs of spiders until they come to investigate – then eat them. This would be a very tiring thing to have to do every day. Not only would you have to wait around for your food, you'd also have to learn to play a web like a harp.

Aim And Spit

Archer fish knock flies into the water by spitting at them. Your parents probably tell you never to spit in public, but they couldn't tell you off if it was the only way you could catch a good meal.

... You Could Eject Your Stomach?

You might not enjoy cooking, but perhaps you should be thankful that preparing your next meal doesn't involve any of the following disgusting practices.

Hard To Stomach

When a starfish finds a shellfish it wants to eat, it ejects its stomach and plonks it directly on top of its victim. If you had this spectacular talent, it probably wouldn't be a great idea to do it at a fancy dinner party – it's a bit worse than slurping your soup.

ROTTEN 4 RATING

Look Out!

A cunning way to catch your dinner would be to copy a bearded vulture. It drops rocks on tortoises from a great height. Imagine your poor victims, one minute they'd be minding their own business and the next thing – SPLAT – boulders would fall on their heads.

Slime, Glorious Slime

Velvet worms squirt slime at their prey. This would be one way to make sure you got the last helping of food – no one would fancy eating slime covered snacks.

... Your Mum Ate Your Dad's Head?

Everyone argues sometimes – mums and dads, brothers and sisters – but in the wild world of animals, some males have to really watch their step or things can get deadly.

Don't Lose Your Head

Isn't it gross when your mum and dad kiss or hold hands? Consider yourself lucky that your mum doesn't have the habits of a type of insect called a praying mantis. After getting romantic, the female sometimes bites off her partner's head. Just be grateful your dad still has his head – some poor praying mantis babies can't say the same about theirs.

SCARY 5 SCORE

All Tied Up

A male lynx spider will tie up a female with his silk to stop her from eating him. What if your dad had to do that whenever he took your mum out?

Dance For Your Life!

Male wolf spiders do special dances that (sometimes) stop the females from eating them. What if your dad had to dance for your mum to make sure he lived to see another day? It might be entertaining for you, but your poor dad wouldn't find it much fun.

... You Ate Your Mum's Skin?

Hopefully you consider your mum more than just a source of delicious meals. Motherhood wouldn't be much fun if kids liked to munch on their mums' bodies at every available chance.

Skinny Supper

Your mum might let you get away with all sorts of naughty things, but what would she say if you decided to take a nibble of her skin? Baby caecilians, which look like worms but are actually related to frogs, survive their first few days of life by eating their mother's skin. She even grows an extra-thick layer of skin for this purpose. Your own mum probably wouldn't thank you for gnawing on her arm while she's trying to read the newspaper.

New Born Gnawers

In some spider species, the first thing babies do after hatching is eat their mother. That's a nice way to thank your poor old mum!

Monster Babies

Probably the most unlucky mother in the animal world is the gall midge (a type of flying insect). Her gruesome babies are so impatient to be born that they eat their way out of her body. Just imagine …

SCARY
5
SCORE

... Your Mum Had A Million Babies?

Your mum might tell you how special you are by saying that you're one in a million, but what if you actually had a million brothers and sisters?

So Many Siblings

There's no doubt about it, brothers and sisters can be extremely annoying. If you're lucky, you might only have one or two, but if you were a mackerel your mum could give birth to anything between 300,000 and 1,500,000 babies – all at the same time. That's a lot of nappy changing and mopping up of dribble for your poor parents.

Back babies

Pregnant Surinam toads carry babies in the skin on their backs. If human women had to carry their babies like this, they'd be forced to walk hunched over as their back bulges got bigger and bigger. On the plus side, once fully grown, the babies can just pop out from the skin on a toad's back. Easy!

More Bizarre Births

- Quails grow up fast. These birds can have babies when they are just six weeks old.

- Greenflies don't need to mate to have babies and are often already pregnant when they are born.

- The common tenrec (a small furry creature from Madagascar) can produce – and successfully look after – 30 babies in one litter.

... You Were Brought Up By A Lion?

When adults want to adopt a baby, it's a human baby they'll be after. Some animals don't seem to care what species they get.

Ferocious Foster Family

Do you ever wish your mum and dad were more interesting? In Kenya, one unusual lioness repeatedly 'adopted' and looked after baby antelopes, which would normally be lunch for a lion. If you were brought up by lions, you'd have a very different life:

- You'd sleep in a thicket or den.
- You would be carried around by the scruff of your neck.
- You'd be at risk of leopard or hyena attacks.
- You might have up to four very ferocious brothers and sisters to play with.

SCARY 4 SCORE

Baby Snatchers

If a female emperor penguin loses her baby, she might attempt to adopt her neighbour's. Luckily humans don't do this, or your mum might try to adopt the kid next door if you were ever late home from school.

Baby-Sitting Bees

Cuckoo bees make bees from other nests look after their babies. Watch out – if you don't behave yourself, your mum might be tempted to dump you and your brothers and sisters off at a stranger's house.

... You Were A Kid Forever?

Just like Peter Pan, wouldn't it be great if you never had to grow up? But think carefully – it could be quite frustrating if no one ever took you seriously.

Kidding Around

Domestic cats can act like kittens for all of their lives. This may be because in the wild their parents would have encouraged them to live on their own, but their human 'parents' don't do this. If you could act like a kid your entire life, you could play in the park all day long, eat ice cream for breakfast and never have to worry about getting a job.

HOW
★ 5 ★
HANDY

Forever Young

When it's a baby, a salamander (a type of amphibian) has gills, which are organs that allow some creatures to breathe underwater. Most salamanders will lose them when they become an adult, but a type of salamander called an axolotl has gills like a baby all its life. Imagine looking like a baby all your life and having to convince everyone you were really an adult.

Growing Pains

The fulmar (a kind of seabird) looks just the same at one year old as it does when it's 50. How tiresome would it be to never look like you are growing even one day older?

... Your Bed Was Made Of Pants?

What would your ideal bed be made of? Soft feathers?
A fluffy cloud? Just count yourself lucky you don't have to
sleep in rotting garbage or old underwear.

Where's The Underwear?

Red kite are birds of prey that like to collect things with
which to decorate their nests. Some have been known
to steal people's underwear to make their nests extra
colourful. If you collected underwear to decorate your
bedroom, your mum probably wouldn't be thrilled if she
opened your door to find a heap of pants where your
bed used to be. She probably gets fed up of picking
up your clothes, let alone other people's that you've
decided to collect.

Spit 'n' Sleep

The edible-nest swiftlet is a small bird that makes a nest from its own spit. The spit dries out to make a solid crust. Would you fancy sleeping in a bed made of your mum and dad's spit?

Cot Of Rot

What if you were born in a pile of rotting garbage? The mallee-fowl (a chicken-like bird) buries its eggs in a big pile of decaying vegetation. The rotting process provides warmth that helps the eggs to hatch. If you were born in a bin, it might be cosy but it would definitely be a bit smelly.

ROTTEN **3** RATING

... **Your Dad Tried To Eat You?**

What's your mum or dad's favourite food? A juicy steak or a tasty pizza? What if their favourite food wasn't food at all – but YOU?

Ferocious Fathers

If you get on your dad's nerves, the worst he might do is tell you to go to your room. Thank your lucky stars you're not a bass fish. A male will sometimes guard his babies carefully for a few days, then suddenly start eating them.

SCARY SCORE 5

Babies For Breakfast

Goldfish eat their own eggs. If you were in danger of being eaten from the moment you popped into the world, you'd really have to rely on a midwife at the hospital to save you from your hungry mum.

Signs Your Mum Is A Panda

If you know any twins, they probably complain when their parents dress them in the same clothes. But if they were brought up by a giant panda, she would pick her favourite and let the other one starve. If you're a twin, make sure you watch out for the following:

- Your mum starts to regularly weigh and measure you and your twin. A panda will size up her twins and select the strongest to live.

- When you wake up, your twin has already been washed, brushed and fed by your mum, and there is only a stale piece of bread left over for you.

- Your house is full of pictures of a cute baby – but it's not you.

- Your mum seems to forget your birthday, even though it's on the same day as your twin's.

- Your twin starts to get more friends than you, because you're becoming a bit dirty and smelly.

... **Your Parents Abandoned You?**

If you have wonderful people who take care of you and tell you how special you are, you should feel very lucky indeed. Some creatures in the animal kingdom are lucky just to have anyone look after them at all.

Are You There, Mum?

If you hatched out of an egg on a deserted beach and your mum was nowhere to be seen, do you think you could find your way home? Turtles bury their eggs in the sand, then leave them there to hatch.
By the time the babies hatch and crawl out of the sand, the mums are long gone. If you ever found yourself in this predicament, let's just hope you had lots of brothers and sisters to help you out.

See Ya!

Swallows migrate to Africa for the winter. If they still have babies in their nests when migration time comes, they will simply leave them. What if your parents went on holiday without you? You'd have the whole house to yourself, could eat as many snacks as you like and watch whatever you like on TV. Brilliant!

Thanks, Mum

Most birds look after their babies for at least a couple of weeks, but megapode chicks have to fend for themselves from day one. Imagine if you'd had to wash your own clothes and cook your own meals as a baby.

HOW HANDY
0

… Your Parents Coated You In Venom?

It's no secret: parents can be extremely embarrassing. If they aren't kissing you in public then they're calling you baby names in front of your friends. Could it get any worse? Yes …

Lethal Lick

A slow loris (a small mammal) has a gland on its arm that oozes venom. It licks up this venom and coats its babies with it to stop them being eaten by predators. If your mum did this to you, it might stop you being munched on, but it certainly wouldn't help you make any friends.

ROTTEN
3
RATING

Follow The Leader

Shrew families travel around in 'caravans', where each baby holds on to the back of the one in front, using its teeth. How would you like it if your little brothers and sisters had to hold on to your T-shirt wherever you went?

Dinner's Ready

Cheetahs bring live baby antelopes to their cubs for them to learn how to chase and kill. If at mealtimes your mum released a live sheep on to the table, you'd either have to learn some cheetah tactics or go hungry.

... You Were Pampered By Everyone?

Having overprotective parents can be irritating, but they only do it because they love you. Try to relax and enjoy the attention and be thankful they don't take things as far as some animals do.

Perfectly Pampered

How would you like to arrive home from school to find your mum, dad, brothers and sisters waiting to attend to your every whim? This is the celebrity treatment that baby moorhens receive. They are lovingly fed and cared for not only by their mums and dads, but also by their older brothers and sisters.

HOW
5
HANDY

The Booby Prize

Male dyak fruit bats are the only male mammals that have milk-producing breasts, so both mums and dads feed their young. Just imagine your own dad with a pair of breasts …

Never Fly The Nest

A baby albatross sits in its nest for nearly a year, being brought food by both parents. This may not seem like a very long time, but baby birds usually leave their nests much earlier. Just try to imagine a grown adult still being cared for like a baby.

... Your Neighbourhood Shared One Toilet?

Humans seem to enjoy living together – it's nice to have a bit of company. But what if you had to share one toilet with loads of people, or you didn't even have your own bed? Nightmare!

Lav Thy Neighbour

Living with a big family might mean you argue over who gets to use the bathroom first in the morning. If this is one of your pet peeves, thank your lucky stars you're not a raccoon. These furry critters share a toilet with all their neighbours. If you had to do the same, not only would you have to wait ages to use it, the smell would be unbearable.

Sleepy Squeezes

On cold winter nights, birds called wrens will squeeze into the same roosting hole for warmth. Up to 34 of them have been seen to go into one nest box together. Would you fancy sharing a bed with 34 people?

One Too Many

Guillemots are birds that nest in huge colonies, packing tightly on to cliff ledges. If there's room to sit down, there's room to have a family. What if all houses on your street had swarms of kids on every windowsill?

... Geeks Got All The Attention?

Everyone wants to be popular, especially at school. Some animals love to be popular, too.

Geek Chic

You should never hide how wonderfully clever you are just to fit in at school. In groups of chimps, the dominant one isn't always bigger and tougher than the others – he is cleverer and better at getting his fellow chimps on his side – especially the females.

SMART
5
POINTS

Popular And Pampered

If you're popular at school, you might get invited to lots of parties or have a load of people trying to talk to you. But if you and your friends lived like meerkats, you'd also be stroked and groomed every morning when you got to school.

Sitting Pretty

Dominant velvet worms sit on top of the lower-ranking members of the group. Be thankful this isn't the way humans treat each other, or some kids would be in danger of spending their lunchtimes being sat on.

... You Built A Tower Of Poo?

You'd probably like your bedroom to be a little bubble of happiness where eagle-eyed parents and nosy brothers and sisters leave you in peace. What's the best way to protect your haven?

Bedroom Watch

A topi (a kind of antelope) produces large piles of poo to mark its territory. It then stands on top of the pile to get a good view of its surroundings. If you did this, not only would you always be able to tell who was sneaking into your bedroom, the horrid smell would also deter any unwelcome visitors.

ROTTEN
5
RATING

Butterfly Security

Male comma butterflies spend all day flying around their territory, attacking anything else that flies past, including other insects and even birds. You might need to employ a whole army to protect your bedroom – or even your whole house – in this way.

Who Needs A Handshake?

When your cat lovingly rubs his head against your leg, he's marking you as part of his territory with his facial scent glands. What if this was how your best friends greeted you at school every day?

... You Could Head Butt Your Rivals?

Violence is never the answer, but try telling that to some of the beastly brutes of the animal world, where rivalry can get very nasty.

Strong As An Ox

Male musk oxen fight their rivals with furious head-butting. This is an incredibly bad idea unless you happen to have the massive head-protecting horns of a musk ox. If you don't, then you had better stick with thumb-wrestling to settle your differences.

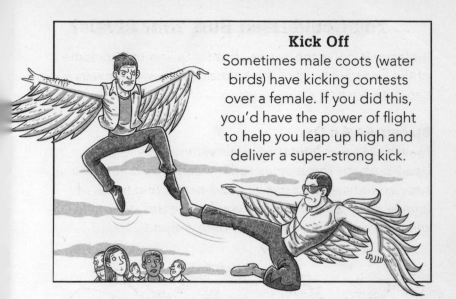

Kick Off

Sometimes male coots (water birds) have kicking contests over a female. If you did this, you'd have the power of flight to help you leap up high and deliver a super-strong kick.

Bloody Bears

By the time polar bears finish their two-week mating season, the males are covered in blood from fighting each other. This might be an attractive look for a polar bear, but it's not a recommended way to impress humans.

SCARY
5
SCORE

... Girls Got First Pick At Lunch?

Boys don't like to admit it, but sometimes they can be pushed around by girls. Some strange animal behaviour, however, takes this one step too far.

Females First

On a boring school day, it's a relief when lunchtime comes around and you get to stuff your face and chill out with your friends. But just imagine if the girls got to eat first. Female spotted hyenas get first pick at every meal a pack enjoys. The boys might be left with only wilted salad to eat. It wouldn't really be fair, would it? Unless you're a girl, of course!

Hello, Up There!

If you're very short, you might find it difficult to get noticed. Female echiurid worms can be a whopping 120 times longer than the male worms. This would be the equivalent of a human woman growing to over 21,000 centimetres tall next to an average sized man. That's twice as tall as the Statue of Liberty. If human women were this tall, it would be terribly scary to be a man. You'd have to be very careful to keep from getting under a woman's feet – they might accidentally squish you.

HOW
1
HANDY

... Girls Did All The Work?

Sometimes, females in the animal world have no choice but to be the ones to take charge because the males of their species are so useless.

Lazy Queens

Ant colonies are ruled by a queen who is bigger than all the worker ants – all of which are also female. The worker ants take care of the queen and her babies. That's like your mum employing the help of a hundred of her female friends to take care of everything for her. The only males in an ant colony are called drones. Drone ants don't do any work at all, so they certainly wouldn't be any help.

Hop On

Sometimes female toads have to give their super-lazy partners a piggyback ride to the pond. If this was the only way human men would go to work, the roads would be full of very annoyed women instead of cars.

More Bossy Ladies

Move over, boys. Let the ladies take control.

- Elephant herds are led by the dominant female. None of the members want to get on the wrong side of her.

- Female birds of prey can be nearly twice as heavy as the males. Now that's really something to squawk about.

- Clownfish live in groups of males, led by one dominant female. Does a male take charge if the female dies? Sure, but he has to change into a female clownfish first.

... You Dressed Up In Feathers?

Some male animals really have to look special if they have any hope of impressing the ladies. But their idea of what looks special might be slightly different from yours.

Fashion Tips From A Peacock

Want to look as fabulous as a peacock? Here's how:

1. Grow a shimmering plumage of green and blue feathers, complete with a spectacularly long tail.

2. When you need the 'wow' factor, display your tail like a huge, swaying fan.

3. Complete the look with a pretty crest on top of your head.

Singing Star

Female great reed warbler birds only choose companions who can sing very complicated songs. They spend several days listening and comparing a few different males before picking a lucky winner. It can be hard enough to impress someone, without having to go through a cringe-worthy talent contest, too.

SMART 3 POINTS

Damsel Disguises

Male ruffs birds can fool other males by looking like females. This way they can sneak closer to the real females without being beaten up by other males. A smart move – if you don't mind dressing like a girl.

SMART 4 POINTS

... You Used A Pebble To Propose?

From presents of pebbles to showers of poo, animals can be very caring. Why not take note of these tips?

Present A Pebble

The best gift a male Adélie penguin can give to his mate is a pebble for her nest. So forget a diamond ring – here's how a suitor could propose like a penguin:

1. He must find a great-looking pebble. It shouldn't be too large or have any sharp edges.

2. The pebble must be taken home for a good polish, then he should decide on the best time and place to surprise that special someone.

3. He should get down on one knee and reveal his pebble in a romantic way.

4. As soon as his special someone sees how shiny and beautiful the pebble is, they will be over the moon.

Feet Friendly

A male tortoise often bites the feet of females to show that he likes them. If human males acted in this way, women would never be able to wear flip-flops again!

Poo Propeller

Male hippos like to shower a mixture of pee and poo over female hippos, spinning their tails like propellers to get a good spray. This might be very touching, but if you did it, you'd have to advise your friends to wear raincoats.

ROTTEN 5 RATING

... Someone Drank Your Pee?

It's fun to make new friends, but would you still feel that way if your new buddy tried to drink your pee? Or if he had a giant claw for a hand?

Pee Pals

It can sometimes be difficult to tell if someone wants to hang out with you or not, but not if you're a giraffe. To decide if a female giraffe fancies hanging out with him, a male tastes her pee. If humans did the same, all they'd need to do is take one sneaky sip and they could save themselves a whole heap of bother.

ROTTEN
3
RATING

Creepy Claws

Having trouble making friends? All you need is a giant claw. One of the male fiddler crab's two claws grows much larger than the other. The male waves his monster claw around and whacks it on the ground to entice females. Human females probably wouldn't appreciate this kind of attention.

Love You And Leaf You

Butterflies don't have great eyesight, and may attempt to befriend dead leaves by mistake. If you find yourself accidentally hugging a leaf, you might need a stronger pair of glasses.

You will also love ...

ISBN: 978-1-906082-18-5

ISBN: 978-1-907151-52-1

ISBN: 978-1-78055-114-2